AF585098

THE COOKBOOK

Creating delicious moments

THE COOKBOOK

Creating delicious moments

CONTENTS

As Executive Chef at Arnott's, I have a dream job helping to create delicious moments with our iconic biscuits. For 160 years, Arnott's has been creating, sharing and making bikkies people enjoy throughout their lives. With this cookbook, we are excited to share some much-loved timeless recipes, as well as some new ones, that you, your friends and your family can enjoy.

These recipes are perfect to recreate at home, using ingredients easily found in your pantry or local supermarket.

This cookbook is particularly special to me as it is a collaboration with the Australian Women's Weekly. My mum, Jennifer, who passed away much too early, was given a Women's Weekly cookbook from her mother-in-law, Pat, which she then passed to me. This quickly became a treasured possession, and from it, I started my own cooking journey, finding comfort and inspiration in its pages.

This is also a tribute to my children, Sophie and Charles. You have always been eager to taste-test, offer your enthusiastic feedback (whether good or bad) and be part of this journey, enjoying a Choc Ripple Cake or two along the way.

To you, the reader, who have helped make Arnott's the iconic bikkie brand it is today, I hope this cookbook helps to create your own special memories, whether you've been enjoying Arnott's biscuits from childhood or if it's your first time biting into one of our delicious bikkies.

Thank you for allowing us to be part of your journey and enjoy the delicious moments ahead!

Chef Ness

The recipes in this book, where relevant, include handy buttons at the top of the page so you can easily identify the following features at a glance:

GF Gluten Free option
MA Make Ahead
FF Family Favourite / (kid) Friendly
NB No Bake

P.S. Want more flavour ideas and expert tips on all things Arnott's? Scan here for even more amazing recipes, hacks and inspiration!

Tiny Teddy These delightful bear-shaped biscuits are the perfect treat for kids (and adults!) any time of the day.

Scotch Finger Loved for its crumbly, melt-in-your-mouth texture and rich buttery taste, they're made to snap and dunk!

Choc Ripple Crafted with cocoa, these biscuits contain no artificial flavours or preservatives, making them ideal for snacking and baking.

KNOW *your* BISCUITS

Gaiety Savour the contrasting textures of crispy wafer and hazelnut-flavoured cream, coated in chocolate for an indulgent treat.

Butternut Snap Delightfully crunchy, this sweet biscuit is made with the deliciousness of oats, coconut and golden syrup.

Tina Wafer Your biscuity best friend! Yummy, light and crispy, cream-filled wafers in scrumptious raspberry, vanilla and chocolate flavours.

Iced VoVo Add a little fancy to your day with these delicate bicuits. Unmistakenly an Australian favourite.

Mint Slice With a smooth chocolate coating and a cool minty centre, this iconic Aussie biscuit is indulgent and irresistible.

Malt 'O' Milk A crunchy sweet biscuit with baked malt notes. It contains no artificial flavours or preservatives.

Arnott's biscuits are truly iconic and have been loved by Australians for generations. What's your favourite?

Raspberry Shortcake The perfect combination of melt-in-your-mouth shortcake, sandwiched with a burst of jammy raspberry-flavoured filling.

TeeVee Snacks Malt Sticks Coated in a layer of smooth chocolate, it melts in your mouth as you bite into its light and crunchy biscuit centre.

Milk Arrowroot Baked light and crunchy for a deliciously simple sweet biscuit, the original biscuit has been trusted since 1888.

ARNOTT
SCOTCH

Everyday
Delicious
MaltoMilk
MaltoMilk
MaltoMilk
MaltoMilk
MaltoMilk

Scotch Finger brownie bars

PREP TIME 20 MINS **COOK TIME** 45 MINS

We love a fudgy brownie, so the cooking time in this recipe will give you just that. If you prefer more of a cakey texture, simply cook the brownie for a further 5 minutes, until the skewer comes out clean.

BISCUIT BASE

250g pkt Arnott's Scotch Finger biscuits

100g unsalted butter, melted

BROWNIE TOPPING

150g dark chocolate Melts

100g unsalted butter, chopped

2 eggs, lightly beaten

135g caster sugar

65g brown sugar

65g plain flour, sifted

1 Preheat oven to 160°C fan-forced.

2 Grease a 20cm square cake tin; line base and sides with baking paper, extending the paper 2cm above edge of tin.

3 Biscuit Base: Place Scotch Finger biscuits in bowl of a food processor and pulse until fine crumbs form. Add melted butter and bake for 20 minutes.

4 Brownie Topping: Place chocolate and butter in a microwave-safe bowl. Microwave for 1–2 minutes on medium power, stirring every 30 seconds until melted and smooth.

5 In a large bowl, combine eggs, caster sugar and brown sugar and mix well. Stir in chocolate mixture. Add sifted flour and mix to combine. Pour mixture over biscuit base and bake for 25 minutes at 170°C fan-forced or until a skewer inserted in the centre comes out slightly damp. Cool in the tin.

6 Cut brownie into bars before serving.

MAKES 12

A TIP FROM
Chef Ness
Store brownie in an airtight container for up to 3 days.

Scotch Finger apple slice

PREP TIME 15 MINS **COOK TIME** 45 MINS

You can't go wrong with this childhood favourite. The apple topping has a light and tangy flavour with notes of cinnamon, combining beautifully with the buttery biscuit base. A recipe worthy of keeping in the family.

BISCUIT BASE

2 x 250g pkts Arnott's Scotch Finger biscuits (or 500g Arnott's Gluten Free Scotch Finger biscuits)

250g unsalted butter, melted

APPLE TOPPING

800g can pie apple slices

300ml sour cream

1 tsp vanilla extract

1½ tbsp cinnamon sugar

1 Preheat oven to 180°C fan-forced.

2 Grease and line a 20cm x 30cm slice tin with baking paper, extending the paper 5cm above edge of tin.

3 Biscuit Base: Place Scotch Finger biscuits in the bowl of a food processor and pulse until fine crumbs form. Add melted butter and pulse until combined. Press mixture firmly into base of tin, smoothing the surface with a spoon or flat-based glass.

4 Apple Topping: Place apple slices on paper towel to absorb moisture.

5 In a large bowl, combine sour cream and vanilla. Fold in apple and spoon onto biscuit base. Top with cinnamon sugar.

6 Bake for 40–45 minutes or until lightly browned. Cool in tin. Cover and refrigerate until ready to serve.

7 Cut into pieces before serving.

MAKES 16

A TIP FROM

Chef Ness

Store slice in an airtight container in the fridge for up to 3 days.

Wagon Wheels brownie cakes

PREP TIME 10 MINS **COOK TIME** 30 MINS

Wagon Wheels are a wonderful chocolate-coated combination of marshmallow, jam and biscuit. Here, they're enveloped in a brownie batter, so you can expect a get a jammy, pillowy crunch in every bite.

190g pkt Arnott's Wagon Wheels Original Minis
150g dark chocolate Melts
100g unsalted butter, chopped
2 eggs
135g caster sugar
65g brown sugar
65g plain flour, sifted
vanilla ice-cream and extra Arnott's Wagon Wheels Original Minis, halved, to serve, optional

1 Preheat oven to 160°C fan-forced.

2 Line a 6-hole (¾ cup) Texas muffin pan with paper cases. Finely chop 2 Wagon Wheels Minis and set aside.

3 Place chocolate and butter in a microwave-safe bowl. Microwave for 1–2 minutes on medium power, stirring every 30 seconds until melted and smooth.

4 In a large bowl, combine eggs, caster sugar and brown sugar, mixing well. Stir in chocolate mixture. Add sifted flour and mix to combine. Stir through reserved chopped biscuits. Divide mixture between paper cases and top each with 1 Wagon Wheels Mini. Bake for 25–30 minutes until cakes spring back when touched. Transfer cakes to a wire rack to cool.

5 Serve cakes topped with ice-cream and an extra half a Wagon Wheels mini.

MAKES 6

Scan here for a short how-to video making this recipe.

A TIP FROM

Chef Ness

Cover cakes with foil for last 5–10 minutes of baking time, so the Wagon Wheels don't overcook.

A TIP FROM

Chef Ness

Feel free to use your family's favourite jam in this recipe.

Choc Ripple coconut slice

PREP TIME 15 MINS **COOK TIME** 25 MINS **FRIDGE TIME** 20 MINS

The perfect treat for morning tea, you'll love the flavours of chocolate, raspberry jam and coconut goodness in every square.

icing sugar (ensure gluten free, if required), to serve

BISCUIT BASE

250g pkt Arnott's Choc Ripple biscuits (or 250g Arnott's Gluten Free Scotch Finger biscuits)

100g unsalted butter, melted

¼ cup (80g) raspberry jam

COCONUT FILLING

⅓ cup (55g) caster sugar

1½ cups (80g) desiccated or shredded coconut

1 egg

30g unsalted butter, melted

1 tbsp milk

½ tsp baking powder (ensure gluten free, if required)

1 Preheat oven to 160°C fan-forced.

2 Grease and line a 20cm square cake tin with baking paper, extending the paper 2cm above edge of tin.

3 Biscuit Base: Place Choc Ripple biscuits in the bowl of a food processor and pulse until fine crumbs form. Add melted butter and pulse until combined. Press mixture firmly into base of tin, smoothing the surface with the back of a spoon or flat-based glass. Refrigerate for 20 minutes or until firm. Spread jam over biscuit base.

4 Coconut Filling: In a bowl, combine all ingredients and mix well. Carefully spoon mixture over jam; using the back of a spoon, smooth the surface of the filling. Bake for 20–25 minutes until golden and firm. Cool in tin.

5 Cut into squares and dust with icing sugar before serving.

MAKES 16

Nice baked cheesecake

PREP TIME 20 MINS **COOK TIME** 1 HR **FRIDGE TIME** 20 MINS

What's the secret to a silky smooth filling? Make sure the cream cheese, eggs and sour cream are all at room temperature before you start.

berries and thick cream, to serve, optional

BISCUIT BASE

250g pkt Arnott's Nice biscuits

125g butter, melted

CREAM CHEESE FILLING

2 x 250g pkts cream cheese, at room temperature

¾ cup (165g) caster sugar

2 tsp finely grated lemon zest

3 eggs

250g sour cream

2 tbsp lemon juice

1 Preheat oven to 150°C fan-forced. Grease and line base of a 22cm (base measure) springform tin.

2 Biscuit Base: Place Nice biscuits in the bowl of a food processor and pulse until fine crumbs form. Add melted butter and pulse until combined. Spoon mixture into tin, press firmly over the base and up the sides, smoothing the surface with the back of a spoon or flat-based glass. Refrigerate for 20 minutes or until firm.

3 Cream Cheese Filling: In the bowl of an electric mixer, beat cream cheese, sugar and lemon zest until well combined. Add eggs, one at a time, beating well after each addition. Add sour cream and lemon juice, beating until combined. Pour mixture over biscuit base. Place tin on an oven tray.

4 Bake for 1 hour or until just set (cake should have a slight jiggle to the filling when gently shaken). Turn oven off and leave cheesecake in the oven with the door ajar until cooled (this helps prevent it from cracking). Cover and refrigerate until ready to serve.

5 Serve slices of cheesecake with berries and thick cream, if you like.

SERVES 10–12

Tim Tam scones

PREP TIME 10 MINS **COOK TIME** 12 MINS

Why not switch up the flavour of these decadent afternoon tea favourites. If you love white chocolate, swap out Tim Tam Original biscuits with Tim Tam White biscuits. Or if caramel is more your thing, use Tim Tam Chewy Caramel biscuits for extra caramel goodness.

5 Arnott's Tim Tam Original biscuits
4 cups (600g) self-raising flour, sifted
300ml thickened cream
300ml lemonade
whipped cream and strawberries, to serve

1 Preheat oven to 200ºC fan-forced. Line a baking tray with baking paper.

2 Roughly chop Tim Tam biscuits.

3 Place flour in a large bowl. Add the cream and lemonade; using a butter knife, stir the mixture until it starts to come together. Add chopped biscuits; stir to combine but don't overmix.

4 Transfer dough onto a work surface and knead gently (see tip), then pat down into a 3cm thick disc.

5 Using a lightly floured 5cm round cutter, cut out rounds. Place on lined tray and bake for 10–12 minutes, or until golden. Cool.

6 Serve scones split in half, topped with whipped cream and strawberries.

MAKES 12

A TIP FROM

Chef Ness

Scones need a light touch, so be mindful not to overknead the dough or the scones may be tough.

Scotch Finger chocolate caramel slice

PREP TIME 15 MINS **COOK TIME** 20 MINS **FRIDGE TIME** 40 MINS

Get ready to dive into layers of buttery biscuits, heavenly caramel and chocolate goodness with this decadent slice recipe. Who can resist?

BISCUIT BASE

250g pkt Arnott's Scotch Finger biscuits (or 250g Arnott's Gluten Free Scotch Finger biscuits)

100g unsalted butter, melted

CARAMEL FILLING

395g can sweetened condensed milk

2 tbsp golden syrup

60g unsalted butter

CHOCOLATE TOPPING

180g dark chocolate, melted

1 tsp vegetable oil

Scan here for a short how-to video making this recipe.

1 Preheat oven to 170°C fan-forced. Grease and line an 18cm x 28cm slice tin, extending paper 2cm above edge of tin.

2 Biscuit Base: Place Scotch Finger biscuits in the bowl of a food processor and pulse until fine crumbs form. Add melted butter and pulse until combined. Press mixture firmly into base of tin, smoothing the surface with a spoon or flat-based glass. Cover and refrigerate for 20 minutes until firm.

3 Caramel Filling: Place condensed milk, golden syrup and butter in a saucepan over medium heat. Cook, stirring, for 8 minutes or until starting to bubble. Spread caramel mixture over biscuit base. Bake for 10–12 minutes or until golden. Remove from oven and allow to cool.

4 Chocolate Topping: Place chocolate and oil in a microwave-safe bowl. Microwave for 1–2 minutes on medium power, stirring every 30 seconds until melted and smooth. Pour over the filling. Cover and refrigerate for 20 minutes or until chocolate is set.

5 Cut slice into squares before serving.

MAKES 24

Bikkie tin cake

PREP TIME 20 MINS **COOK TIME** 40 MINS

A fun way to use up any leftover biscuits sitting in the biscuit tin, if that ever happens at your place. Use any non-chocolate Arnott's biscuit variety you like. We used Cream Favourites Assorted Biscuits here.

150g butter, softened
¾ cup (165g) caster sugar
1 tsp vanilla extract
2 eggs
2 cups (300g) self-raising flour, sifted
½ cup (125ml) milk
18 leftover Arnott's biscuits such as Cream Favourites Assorted Biscuits

1 Preheat oven to 160°C fan-forced. Grease an 18cm x 28cm slice tin; line base and sides with baking paper, extending the paper 5cm above edge of tin.

2 In the bowl of an electric mixer, beat butter, sugar and vanilla until light and fluffy. Beat in eggs, one at a time.

3 Stir in flour and milk in two batches, alternately. Spread mixture into tin; smooth the surface. Place biscuits on their side in the batter, pushing in gently.

4 Bake for 20 minutes until lightly browned. Cover loosely with foil, cook for a further 15–20 minutes until a skewer inserted in centre comes out clean. Stand in tin for 10 minutes. Transfer to a wire rack to cool.

5 Cut into slices before serving.

SERVES 12

Raspberry Shortcake parfait

PREP TIME 15 MINS **COOK TIME** 10 MINS

Pretty as a picture, these individual layered desserts are simply 'parfait'! With freshness in every spoonful, serve after a lovely springtime lunch.

RASPBERRY COULIS
200g fresh or frozen raspberries, plus extra to serve
½ cup (110g) caster sugar
BISCUIT BASE
250g Arnott's Raspberry Shortcake biscuits
MARSHMALLOW FILLING
150g pink marshmallows
1 tbsp milk
300ml thickened cream

1 Raspberry Coulis: Place raspberries and sugar in a small saucepan over medium heat and cook until the sugar dissolves. Simmer for 5 minutes until raspberries collapse and mixture thickens. Cool for 15 minutes, then cover and refrigerate until ready to serve.

2 Biscuit Base: Reserve 4 Raspberry Shortcake biscuits. Place remaining 10 biscuits in the bowl of a food processor and pulse until crumbs form. Set aside.

3 Marshmallow Filling: Place marshmallows and milk in a small saucepan, stir over low heat for 5 minutes or until melted and mixture is smooth. Transfer to a heatproof bowl. Set aside for 10 minutes to cool, stirring occasionally.

4 In the bowl of an electric mixer, beat cream until firm peaks form. Stir two-thirds of the whipped cream into cooled marshmallow mixture until combined.

5 Spoon crumbs into the base of four 1 cup (250ml) capacity serving glasses. Top with marshmallow filling, raspberry coulis and remaining whipped cream.

6 Serve parfaits topped with extra raspberries and a reserved biscuit.

SERVES 4

A TIP FROM
Chef Ness

To avoid the marshmallow filling splitting, have cream at room temperature before adding.

SAO vanilla slice

PREP TIME 20 MINS **COOK TIME** 5 MINS **FRIDGE TIME** 3 HRS+

This easy vanilla slice is also quick to make. Remember, when making the custard filling, it's important to continually stir the custard while it's simmering to make sure it stays silky smooth and free of any lumps.

BISCUIT BASE
250g pkt Arnott's SAO biscuits

CUSTARD FILLING
90g cornflour
50g custard powder
1 cup (220g) caster sugar
3 cups (750ml) milk
300ml thickened cream
60g butter, chopped
1 tsp vanilla bean paste
3 egg yolks, lightly beaten

PASSIONFRUIT ICING
1½ cups (240g) icing sugar
2 tbsp passionfruit pulp
15g butter, softened

1 Grease a 20cm x 30cm slice tin, line base and sides with baking paper, extending the paper 5cm over the edges.

2 Biscuit Base: Place half the SAO biscuits on base of tin, trimming as necessary to neatly fit.

3 Custard Filling: Combine cornflour, custard powder and sugar in a medium saucepan. Gradually stir in milk and cream, whisking until smooth. Stir continuously over medium-low heat until custard comes to the boil. Reduce heat and simmer, stirring, for 3 minutes until mixture is thick and smooth. Whisk in butter. Remove from heat. Gently whisk in vanilla and egg yolks until smooth.

4 Spread filling evenly over SAO biscuits. Top with remaining biscuits, trimming as necessary to fit. Cover and refrigerate for at least 3 hours or until set.

5 Passionfruit Icing: Combine icing sugar, pulp and butter in a heatproof bowl, stirring over a pan of simmering water, until the icing is smooth and glossy. Pour icing evenly over SAO biscuits. Refrigerate for 20 minutes until set.

6 Cut into squares before serving.

MAKES 12

4 ways Ice-cream sandwiches

Jatz

Place 12 Jatz on a tray. Top each Jatz with a scoop of ice-cream, smooth side and top, sandwich ice-cream with another Jatz and press firmly. Freeze for 20 minutes. Dip each sandwich halfway into a bowl of melted dark chocolate, then dip the chocolate half into a bowl of 100's & 1000's sprinkles to coat. Freeze until ready to serve.

MAKES 12

Malt 'O' Milk

Line a 20cm square cake tin with baking paper. Spoon 1 litre softened Neapolitan ice-cream in distinct colour rows into tin. Place 12 Malt 'O' Milk biscuits on ice-cream in rows. Freeze until firm. Cut around the biscuits. Place another biscuit on the other side of ice-cream to form sandwiches, press firmly, place on a tray and freeze. Dip the end of each sandwich in melted dark chocolate, then dip into crushed nuts. Freeze until ready to serve. MAKES 12

Wagon Wheels

Using a sharp knife split 2 x 48g Arnott's Wagon Wheels biscuits in half to separate. Place 2 biscuits chocolate-side down on a baking-paper-lined tray. Put a round cutter on each biscuit and fill with softened vanilla ice-cream; smooth top. Remove cutter and sandwich with remaining biscuit halves marshmallow-side down, pressing firmly. Freeze until ready to serve. MAKES 2

Scan here for a short how-to video making a Wagon Wheels ice-cream sandwich.

Iced VoVo

Line an 18cm x 28cm slice tin with baking paper. In a bowl, gently combine 1 litre softened vanilla ice-cream with 1 cup (150g) frozen raspberries. Spoon mixture into tin. Place 16 Iced VoVo biscuits on ice-cream in rows. Freeze until firm. Cut around the biscuits. Place another biscuit on the other side of ice-cream to form sandwiches, press firmly. Freeze until ready to serve. MAKES 16

A TIP FROM

Chef Ness

Store slice in an airtight container in the fridge for up to 3 days.

Choc Ripple hazelnut slice

PREP TIME 20 MINS **COOK TIME** 40 MINS **FRIDGE TIME** 20 MINS

Who doesn't love a fudgy roasted hazelnut filling nestled between layers of delectable chocolate! This slice will be on high rotation at your house.

BISCUIT BASE

250g pkt Arnott's Choc Ripple Biscuits

100g butter, melted

HAZELNUT FILLING

4 egg whites

¾ cup (165g) caster sugar

½ cup (70g) roasted hazelnuts, finely chopped

2 tbsp plain flour

1 tbsp cocoa powder

CHOCOLATE TOPPING

180g dark chocolate, chopped

125g unsalted butter, softened

¼ cup (65g) caster sugar

4 egg yolks

1 Preheat oven to 180°C fan-forced. Grease and line a 20cm x 30cm slice tin with baking paper, extending the paper 5cm above edge of tin.

2 Biscuit Base: Place Choc Ripple biscuits in the bowl of a food processor and pulse until fine crumbs form. Add melted butter and pulse until combined. Press mixture firmly into base of tin, smoothing the surface with a spoon or flat-based glass. Refrigerate for 20 minutes or until firm.

3 Hazelnut Filling: In the bowl of an electric mixer, beat egg whites until soft peaks form. Add caster sugar, 1 spoonful at a time, beating well between additions. Beat for 8 minutes or until sugar dissolves and meringue is smooth and glossy. Fold in the hazelnuts, sifted flour and cocoa. Spread filling over the biscuit base. Bake for 20 minutes until firm. Remove from oven, cool in tin for 20 minutes. Reduce oven temperature to 160°C fan-forced.

4 Chocolate Topping: Place chocolate in a microwave-safe bowl. Microwave for 2–3 minutes on medium power, stirring every 30 seconds until melted and smooth. In the bowl of an electric mixer, beat butter, sugar and egg yolks until light and fluffy. Stir in melted chocolate. Spread topping over hazelnut filling. Bake for a further 20 minutes. Cool in tin.

5 Cut into pieces before serving.

MAKES 18

FF

S'mores 3 ways

PREP TIME 10 MINS **COOK TIME** 5 MINS

S'mores are a classic camping treat. Place a marshmallow on a skewer and toast lightly over an open flame until just charred. Sandwich between two of your favourite Arnott's biscuits filled with a piece of chocolate.

MALT 'O' MILK S'MORES
20 Arnott's Malt 'O' Milk biscuits
2 x 100g blocks milk chocolate, broken into squares
20 white marshmallows

JATZ S'MORES
20 Jatz biscuits
100g block dark chocolate, broken into squares
10 pink marshmallows

MARIE ROYAL S'MORES
20 Arnott's Marie biscuits
10 Arnott's Royal biscuits

Scan here for a short how-to video making the Malt 'O' Milk S'mores.

1 Preheat oven to 180°C fan-forced. Line three oven trays with baking paper.

2 Malt 'O' Milk S'mores: Place 10 Malt 'O' Milk biscuits, smooth-side up, on a tray. Top each biscuit with 2 squares of chocolate and 2 marshmallows.

3 Jatz S'mores: Place 10 Jatz biscuits on another tray. Top each biscuit with 1 square of chocolate and 1 marshmallow.

4 Marie Royal S'mores: Place 10 Marie biscuits, smooth-side up, on third tray. Top each biscuit with 1 Royal biscuit. Bake for 5–6 minutes.

5 Meanwhile, place the Malt 'O' Milk and Jatz trays in the oven; bake for 2 minutes until marshmallows start to soften. Remove these trays from oven. Top each with its remaining corresponding biscuits, pressing down gently to stick. Return to oven for a further 1–2 minutes until marshmallow and chocolate are gooey.

6 Remove all three trays from oven. For Marie Royal tray, top each with remaining Marie biscuits. Serve s'mores immediately.

MAKES 30

Tim Tam pikelets

PREP TIME 10 MINS **COOK TIME** 15 MINS

Elevate the simple pikelet by adding chopped Tim Tam biscuits — a great recipe to make with the whole family.

5 Arnott's Tim Tam Original biscuits
1 cup (150g) self-raising flour
1 tbsp caster sugar
pinch of salt
¾ cup (180ml) milk
1 egg
20g butter

1 Roughly chop Tim Tam biscuits and set aside.

2 In a medium bowl, combine flour, sugar and salt, whisking to mix well.

3 Whisk milk and egg together in a jug. Pour milk mixture into the centre of the dry ingredients and gently whisk to form a batter. Stir in chopped Tim Tams.

4 Melt 1 teaspoon of the butter in a non-stick frying pan over medium heat. Spoon tablespoons of batter into pan. Cook pikelets for 1–2 minutes until bubbles appear on the surface. Flip over and cook for a further 1 minute or until browned and cooked through. Remove from pan. Repeat cooking in batches with remaining butter and batter to make 16 pikelets in total.

MAKES 16

Simple
Celebrations

Iced VoVo pavlova

PREP TIME 15 MINS **COOK TIME** 1 HR 30 MINS

The perfect collaboration between two great Aussie icons, this dessert will be an absolute crowd pleaser at your next outdoor gathering.

600ml thickened cream
mint leaves, to serve

PAVLOVA
6 egg whites
1½ cups (330g) caster sugar
2 tsp cornflour
1¼ tsp white vinegar
210g pkt Arnott's Iced VoVo biscuits
½ tsp pink food colouring

RASPBERRY COULIS
250g frozen raspberries
2 tbsp caster sugar

1 Preheat oven to 120°C fan-forced. Mark a 20cm x 30cm rectangle on a sheet of baking paper; place paper marked-side down on an oven tray.

2 Pavlova: In the bowl of an electric mixer, beat egg whites until soft peaks form. Add sugar 1 spoonful at a time, beating well between each addition. Beat for 10 minutes or until sugar dissolves and meringue is smooth and glossy. Add cornflour and vinegar, stir gently to combine.

3 Chop half the Iced VoVo biscuits, reserve remaining biscuits. Add pink food colouring and chopped biscuits to meringue, use a large metal spoon to fold in biscuits until combined. Spread mixture inside the marked rectangle.

4 Bake for 1½ hours or until shell is crisp, pale golden and dry to touch. Turn off oven and leave pavlova in the oven with the door ajar until cooled.

5 Raspberry Coulis: Combine raspberries and sugar In a medium saucepan, cook over medium heat and bring to the boil. Reduce heat and simmer for 5 minutes or until berries are soft. Remove from heat to cool completely. Pass raspberry mixture through a sieve. Set aside.

6 Just before serving, in the bowl of an electric mixer, whisk cream until firm peaks form.

7 Transfer pavlova to a serving plate, cut or break reserved Iced VoVo biscuits into large pieces. Spread whipped cream over pavlova, top with biscuit pieces and drizzle with coulis, then decorate with mint leaves.

SERVES 8–10

Scotch Finger & berry ice-cream cake

PREP TIME 15 MINS **FREEZER TIME** 12 HRS+

The ideal summer celebration dessert. It's best to make it a day ahead so the layers are completely frozen. Take it out of the freezer about 5 minutes before serving to soften slightly, making it easier to cut into slices.

250g pkt Arnott's Scotch Finger biscuits (or 250g Arnott's Gluten Free Scotch Finger biscuits)
100g unsalted butter, melted
600ml thickened cream
395g can sweetened condensed milk
1 cup (150g) frozen mixed berries
fresh mixed berries, cherrries and icing sugar (ensure gluten free, if required), to serve

1 Line a 6cm x 13cm x 24cm loaf tin with baking paper, extending the paper 2cm above edge of tin.

2 Place Scotch Finger biscuits in the bowl of a food processor and pulse until fine crumbs form. Add melted butter and pulse until combined. Press a third of the biscuit mixture firmly into base of tin. Cover and refrigerate until needed. Reserve remaining biscuit crumbs.

3 In the bowl of an electric mixer, beat cream and condensed milk for 3–4 minutes or until firm peaks form.

4 Spoon half the cream mixture over biscuit base. Layer with frozen mixed berries, pressing gently into cream mixture, then top with half the remaining biscuit crumbs, pressing down gently. Spoon remaining ice-cream over biscuit crumbs, smooth top; finish layering with remaining biscuit crumbs, pressing down gently. Cover and freeze for 12 hours or overnight until firm.

5 To serve, turn ice-cream cake out onto a platter, top with fresh mixed berries and cherries. Dust with icing sugar.

SERVES 8–10

Tim Tam ice-cream pudding

PREP TIME 10 MINS **FREEZER TIME** 12 HRS+

For a hot summer Christmas your guests will love this cool alternative to steamed pudding. It's simple to prepare and perfect to make ahead of time. Keep it in the freezer until you're ready to add the final touches and serve.

200g pkt Tim Tam Original biscuits
600ml thickened cream
395g can sweetened condensed milk
1 cup (150g) frozen raspberries
½ cup (125ml) Ice Magic Chocolate
fresh raspberries, to serve

1 Line an 8-cup (2-litre) pudding tin with cling wrap, extending the wrap 5cm over edge of tin.

2 Reserve 2 Tim Tam biscuits. Roughly chop remaining biscuits and set aside.

3 In the bowl of an electric mixer, whisk cream and condensed milk for 3 minutes or until firm peaks form. Add frozen raspberries and chopped biscuits; stir well to combine. Spoon mixture into pudding tin, smooth the top. Cover and freeze for 12 hours or overnight.

4 Coarsely chop reserved biscuits. To serve, turn ice-cream pudding out onto a platter and top with Ice Magic, fresh raspberries and chopped biscuits.

SERVES 10

Scan here for a short how-to video making this recipe.

A TIP FROM

Chef Ness

Prepare ice-cream pudding 1 day ahead to ensure it will be fully frozen when ready to serve. Remove from the freezer 5 minutes before serving to thaw slightly for easy slicing.

A TIP FROM

Chef Ness

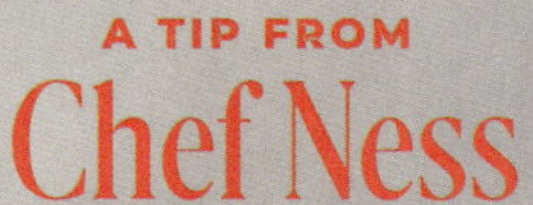

Use any nuts or dried fruit your family loves. Rocky road will keep in an airtight container for up to 5 days.

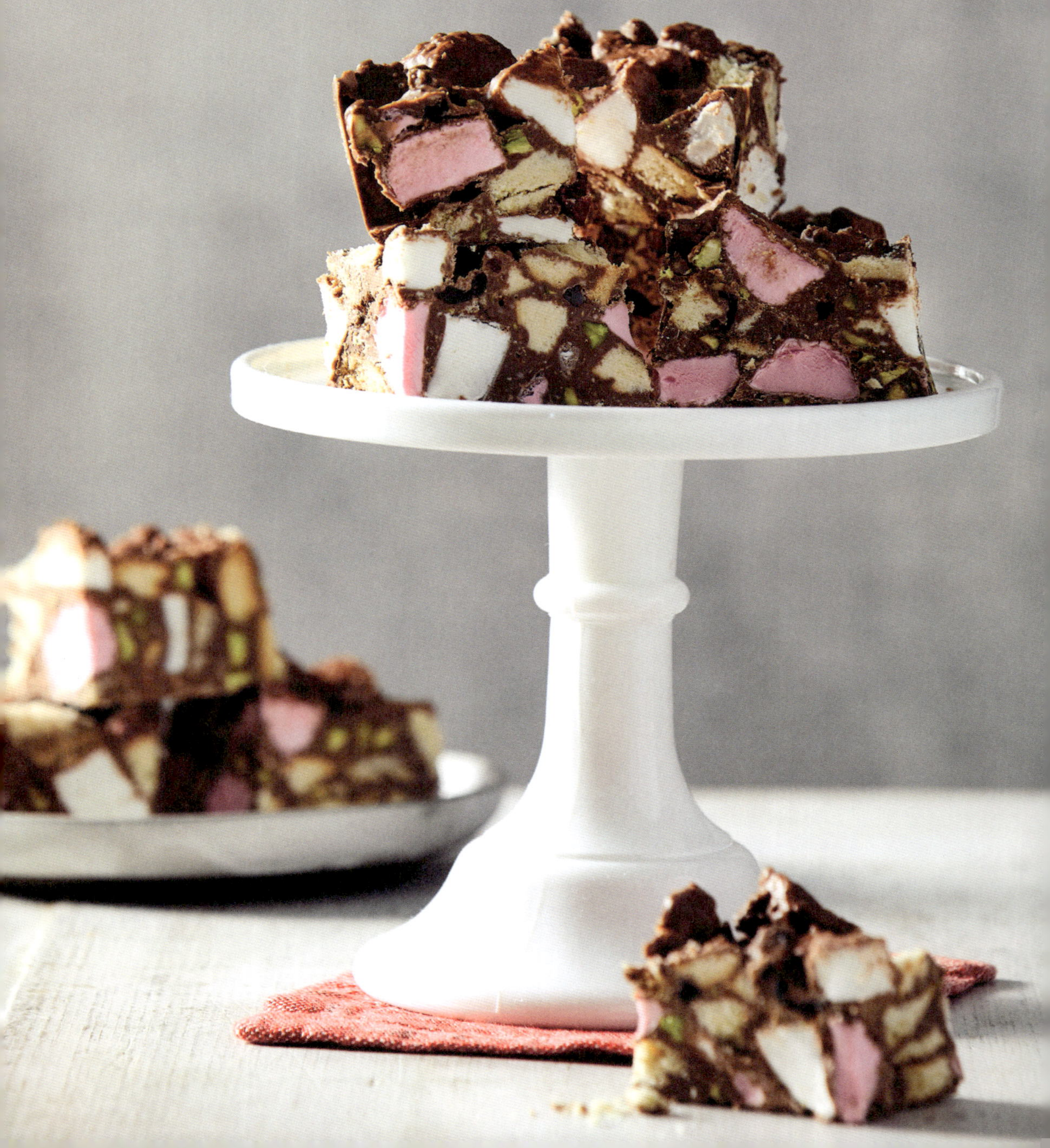

Scotch Finger rocky road

PREP TIME 10 MINS **COOK TIME** 3 MINS **FRIDGE TIME** 2 HRS

This delightfully more-ish rocky road recipe uses half a packet of Arnott's Scotch Finger biscuits. A family favourite, it will disappear in no time, so you may as well make a second batch and use the full packet.

3 x 180g blocks milk chocolate, chopped
125g (½ pkt) Arnott's Scotch Finger biscuits, coarsely chopped
200g marshmallows, halved
⅓ cup (45g) pistachios, coarsely chopped
¼ cup (35g) dried cranberries
¼ cup (20g) desiccated coconut

1 Lightly grease and line a 20cm square cake tin extending the paper 2cm above edge of tin.

2 Place chocolate in a medium microwave-safe bowl. Microwave for 2–3 minutes on medium power, stirring every 30 seconds until melted and smooth. Add remaining ingredients to chocolate and stir well until combined.

3 Spoon mixture evenly into tin. Cover and refrigerate for 2 hours until firm.

4 Cut into squares, before serving.

MAKES 16

Scan here for a short how-to video making this recipe.

Milk Arrowroot reindeers

PREP TIME 30 MINS **COOK TIME** 2 MINS

Create these adorable reindeer faces as a fun, festive activity with the kids. And Santa is sure to love a couple of these left out with a glass of milk.

- 290g pkt white chocolate Melts
- 250g pkt Arnott's Milk Arrowroot biscuits
- 60 Arnott's Tiny Teddy Chocolate biscuits
- 60 candy eyes
- 30 red chocolate buttons

1 Place white chocolate in a microwave-safe bowl. Microwave for 1–2 minutes on medium power, stirring every 30 seconds until melted and smooth.

2 Using a spoon, spread melted white chocolate over the flat side of each Milk Arrowroot biscuit, leaving a 3mm border. Place Tiny Teddy biscuits, face-side down, in the top third of chocolate for antlers. Position 2 candy eyes and 1 red chocolate button for the nose to each biscuit. Stand for 30 minutes or until set.

MAKES 30

A TIP FROM
Chef Ness

Store reindeer biscuits in an airtight container for up to 3 days.

A TIP FROM

Chef Ness

Pavlova can be baked a day ahead; store in an airtight container in a cool dry place. Assemble pavlova close to serving to prevent it going soft.

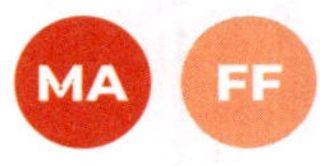

Dark Tim Tam pavlova

PREP TIME 15 MINS **COOK TIME** 2 HRS

While this recipe is all about dark chocolate, you could easily decorate the pavlova with other Tim Tam biscuit flavours if you prefer, such as Tim Tam Original or Tim Tam White.

100g dark chocolate
300ml double cream, whipped

PAVLOVA

200g pkt Arnott's Dark Tim Tam biscuits
6 egg whites
1½ cups (330g) caster sugar
1 tbsp cocoa powder, sifted
2 tsp cornflour, sifted
1¼ tsp white vinegar

1 Preheat oven to 150°C fan-forced. Mark a 20cm circle on a sheet of baking paper; place paper marked-side down on an oven tray.

2 Pavlova: Chop 6 Tim Tams, set aside. Reserve remaining biscuits. In the bowl of an electric mixer, beat egg whites until soft peaks form. Add caster sugar, 1 spoonful at a time, beating well between each addition. Beat for 10 minutes or until sugar dissolves and meringue is smooth and glossy.

3 Add sifted cocoa, cornflour and vinegar to meringue, beat on low speed until combined. Add chopped biscuits, use a large metal spoon to fold biscuits into meringue until just combined. Spread mixture inside marked circle.

4 Bake for 20 minutes, then reduce oven temperature to 120°C fan-forced. Bake for a further 1 hour and 40 minutes or until shell is pale, crisp and dry to touch. Turn oven off, leave pavlova in the oven with door ajar until cooled.

5 Place chocolate in a microwave-safe bowl. Microwave for 1–2 minutes on medium power, stirring every 30 seconds until melted and smooth.

6 Cut reserved Tim Tams in half on the diagonal.

7 To serve, place pavlova on a serving plate, spoon cream on top and decorate with halved Tim Tams, then drizzle with melted chocolate.

SERVES 8

Ginger Nut earl grey trifle

PREP TIME 25 MINS **FRIDGE TIME** 8 HRS+

Fresh tropical flavours combine with layers of gingery biscuits and luscious creamy filling for a tea-lover's delight.

430g can crushed pineapple, drained

CREAM FILLING

300ml thickened cream

2 tsp caster sugar

1 tsp ground ginger

BISCUIT LAYER

250g pkt Arnott's Ginger Nut biscuits

1 cup (250ml) hot, strong earl grey tea

½ cup (70g) pistachios, toasted and finely chopped

1 Cream Filling: In the bowl of an electric mixer, whisk cream, sugar and ginger until firm peaks form. Spread 2 teaspoons of cream mixture over the base of 6 serving glasses.

2 Biscuit Layer: Soak 1 Ginger Nut biscuit in hot tea for 2–3 seconds then place in a serving glass, pressing gently into cream. Sprinkle a few pistachios around the outside of the biscuit then spread with another 2 teaspoons cream mixture and sprinkle with pistachios. Repeat layering with 2 more biscuits, cream filling and pistachios, finishing with a cream filling layer. Repeat layering in remaining glasses. Reserve remaining biscuit.

3 Cover trifles with plastic wrap and refrigerate for 8 hours or overnight to allow biscuits to soften.

4 To serve, coarsely crush the remaining biscuit. Divide pineapple among glasses and top with crushed biscuit.

SERVES 6

A TIP FROM

Chef Ness

Trifles need to be refrigerated overnight to ensure biscuits soften. Use fresh or canned pineapple to decorate the trifles.

A TIP FROM

Chef Ness

Swap the easter eggs for coloured chocolate buttons or chocolate clinkers for an any-time-of-the-year treat.

Scotch Finger Easter fudge

PREP TIME 20 MIN **COOK TIME** 10 MINS **FRIDGE TIME** 4 HRS+

Hop into Easter (or any other occasion) with this delicious fudge recipe. Indulge in the irresistible combination of buttery biscuits and creamy, white chocolate fudge. It's sure to be a favourite for any sweet-tooth.

250g pkt Arnott's Scotch Finger biscuits (or 250g Arnott's Gluten Free Scotch Finger biscuits)
60g butter
500g white chocolate Melts
395g can sweetened condensed milk
125g pkt speckled eggs (or gluten free alternative, if required)

1 Grease and line a 20cm square slice tin with baking paper, extending the paper 2cm above edge of tin.

2 Roughly chop Scotch Finger biscuits. Reserve ⅓ cup chopped biscuits.

3 Place butter, chocolate and condensed milk in a saucepan. Cook over low heat, stirring continually, so it doesn't stick, for 5 minutes or until butter melts and mixture is combined. Continue to cook, stirring, for a further 4–5 minutes until it is just beginning to simmer and mixture is thick and glossy.

4 Remove pan from heat, add chopped biscuits and stir well. Pour mixture into prepared tin, top with speckled eggs and reserved chopped biscuits. Cover and refrigerate for 4 hours or until firm.

5 Cut into squares before serving.

MAKES 24

Scan here for a short how-to video making this recipe.

Jatz board with 2 dips

PREP TIME 30 MINS

Raise your snack game to new heights with these two delicious dips, served with classic Jatz! Enjoy the rich, cream cheese base, topped with smoked salmon and capers on one and a swirl of pesto through the other.

2 x 250g pkts Spreadable Cream Cheese
⅔ cup (160g) ricotta
2 tbsp lemon juice
2 x 225g pkts Arnott's Jatz
baby heirloom carrots, baby cucumbers and asparagus spears, to serve

SMOKED SALMON TOPPING

1 small red onion (100g), thinly sliced
1 tbsp lemon juice
½ teaspoon caster sugar
100g smoked salmon, torn into pieces
1 tbsp baby capers
1 tbsp chopped dill

PESTO DIP

¾ cup basil pesto

1 Place cream cheese, ricotta and lemon juice in the bowl of a food processor, process until smooth, season with salt and pepper. Divide the mixture between two serving bowls.

2 Smoked Salmon Topping: In a small bowl, combine onion with lemon juice, sugar and a large pinch of salt. Set aside for 30 minutes to soften. Drain. On one bowl of cream cheese mixture, top with smoked salmon, capers, drained pickled onion and dill.

3 Pesto Dip: In second bowl of cream cheese mixture, add pesto and swirl it through.

4 Serve dips with Jatz, baby carrots, baby cucumbers and asparagus spears.

SERVES 8

Scan here for a short how-to video making the smoked salmon dip.

4 ways Salada cracks

Dark chocolate

Caramilk

Crack base

PREP TIME 10 MINS **COOK TIME** 20 MINS **MAKES** 20

Preheat oven to 180°C fan-forced. Line a 30cm x 40cm baking tray with foil, then baking paper. Arrange 12 Arnott's Salada crackers over base of tray (3 down, 4 across). Place 220g unsalted butter and 1 cup (220g) brown sugar in a medium saucepan, stir over low heat for 3–5 minutes until butter melts and sugar dissolves. Increase heat, bring to the boil; cook for 3 minutes or until thickened slightly. Remove from heat, stir in 1 tsp vanilla extract. Pour mixture over crackers; working quickly, spread evenly to cover. Bake for 6–8 minutes until golden and bubbling. Stand 5 minutes before spreading with one of the Toppings opposite. Stand until set, then break into pieces.

Scan here for a short how-to video making Caramilk crack.

Valentine's Day

Milk chocolate & sprinkles

Toppings

Valentine's Day Melt 2 x 290g pkts white chocolate Melts in the microwave. Spread two-thirds of the melted chocolate over crack base. Stir a few drops red gel food colour into remaining chocolate to make it pink. Spoon dollops of the pink chocolate over white chocolate, spread and use a skewer to swirl the colours together. Sprinkle with heart-shaped sprinkles.

Milk chocolate & sprinkles Spread 400g melted milk chocolate over crack base. Sprinkle with 100's & 1000's sprinkles.

Caramilk Spread 400g melted white chocolate over crack base. Drizzle with 100g melted caramilk then use a skewer to feather it through the white chocolate.

Dark chocolate Spread 400g melted dark chocolate over crack base.

Scan here for a short how-to video making Valentine's Day crack.

Butternut Snap mango cheesecake

PREP TIME 30 MINS **FRIDGE TIME** 4 HRS+

Celebrate summer with the tropical tastes of mango and coconut, in this luscious cheesecake tart. You'll get a burst of sunshine in every bite.

sliced mango and toasted shredded coconut, extra, to serve

COCONUT BISCUIT BASE

250g pkt Arnott's Butternut Snap Cookies
½ cup (40g) shredded coconut
100g butter, melted

MANGO FILLING

150g chopped fresh mango
1 tbsp caster sugar
1 tsp gelatine powder
1 tbsp boiling water

CREAM CHEESE FILLING

1½ tsp gelatine powder
2 tbsp boiling water
250g pkt cream cheese, softened
⅓ cup (75g) caster sugar
1 tsp vanilla extract
½ cup (125ml) thickened cream

1 Line base of a 12cm x 34cm loose-based tart tin with baking paper.

2 Coconut Biscuit Base: Chop 50g Butternut Snap biscuits and reserve. Place remaining 200g biscuits and coconut in the bowl of a food processor and pulse until fine crumbs form. Add melted butter and process until just combined. Press mixture firmly into base and sides of tin, smoothing the surface. Cover and refrigerate for 20 minutes or until firm.

3 Mango Filling: Place mango and sugar in the bowl of a food processor and process until smooth. Combine gelatine and boiling water in a small jug; stir until gelatine dissolves. Whisk into mango mixture. Refrigerate until it thickens to the consistency of thickened cream.

4 Cream Cheese Filling: Combine gelatine and boiling water in a small jug; stir until gelatine dissolves. In the bowl of an electric mixer, beat cream cheese, sugar and vanilla until smooth. Gradually add cream beating until combined and slightly thickened. Add gelatine mixture beating gently to combine; don't overbeat.

5 Spoon cream cheese filling into biscuit case. Dollop spoonfuls of mango filling on top and, using a skewer, swirl gently through cream cheese filling. Cover and refrigerate for 4 hours or until firm.

6 Serve cheesecake topped with extra sliced mango and toasted coconut, sprinkled with reserved chopped biscuits.

SERVES 12

A TIP FROM

Chef Ness

This cheesecake can also be made in a 24cm round, loose-based tart tin. Store in an airtight container in the fridge for up to 3 days.

Choc Ripple cherry loaf

PREP TIME 25 MINS **FRIDGE TIME** 8 HRS+

Made with just a few ingredients, this classic flavour pairing of chocolate and cherry makes this dessert a favourite for all ages and any occasion. Cut the loaf on the diagonal so each serving gets a layered effect.

600ml thickened cream
2 tsp vanilla extract
2 x 250g pkts Arnott's Choc Ripple biscuits
fresh cherries and toasted coconut flakes, to serve

1 In the bowl of an electric mixer, beat 450ml of the cream with vanilla until firm peaks form.

2 Line a 6.5cm x 13cm x 24cm loaf tin with cling wrap. Spread ⅓ cup of the whipped cream over base of the tin. Place 8 Choc Ripple biscuits on the cream in the tin and spread with a little more cream. Spread 1½ teaspoons of cream on the base of a biscuit then sandwich with the top of another biscuit. Place on its side on top of the base biscuits, running lengthways to form a log. Repeat until all the biscuits have been used to form two logs running side-by-side.

3 Spread the remaining whipped cream over the completed loaf. Cover and refrigerate for 8 hours or overnight to allow the biscuits to soften.

4 Close to serving, in the bowl of an electric mixer beat the remaining cream until firm peaks form. Turn loaf out onto a serving plate and spread cream all over.

5 To serve, top loaf with fresh cherries and toasted coconut.

SERVES 12

Arnott's Easter basket

PREP TIME 1 HR **COOK TIME** 5 MINS

Cute-as-a-button, these adorable bunny and Easter egg designs are the perfect way to decorate these classic Arnott's sweet biscuits.

290g pkt white chocolate Melts
250g pkt Arnott's Milk Arrowroot Biscuits
250g pkt Arnott's Marie biscuits
150g dark chocolate Melts

BUNNY FACES

15 Chocolate Clinkers, halved lengthwise
30 candy eyes
2 tbsp colours of the rainbow sprinkles

BUNNY BOTTOMS

30 Arnott's Tiny Teddy Honey biscuits
15 pink and white mini marshmallows, halved
15 pink and white marshmallows, halved

EASTER EGGS

⅓ cup colours of the rainbow sprinkles

1 Place white chocolate in a microwave-safe bowl. Microwave for 1–2 minutes on medium power, stirring every 30 seconds until melted and smooth.

2 Bunny Faces: Using a spoon, spread one-third of the melted chocolate evenly over half the Milk Arrowroot biscuits leaving a 3mm border. Place 2 clinkers halves on the top quarter of chocolate for ears, position 2 candy eyes and scatter with rainbow sprinkles.

3 Bunny Bottoms: Spread remaining white chocolate over the Marie biscuits, leaving a 3mm border. Place 2 Tiny Teddy biscuits face-side down, angled slightly inwards towards the bottom third of the biscuit. Dollop each Tiny Teddy with a little melted chocolate and top with a mini marshmallow half. Place a halved marshmallow in the centre of biscuit.

4 Easter Eggs: Place the dark chocolate in a microwave-safe bowl. Microwave for 1–2 minutes on medium power, stirring every 30 seconds until melted and smooth. Spread dark chocolate over the remaining Arrowroot biscuits, leaving a 3mm border. Sprinkle with rainbow sprinkles as you like.

MAKES 60

A TIP FROM

Chef Ness

Store these biscuits in an airtight container for up to 3 days.

A TIP FROM
Chef Ness

The pie can be made to the end of step 4, 1 day ahead and stored in the fridge. The lemon flavour will intensify overnight. Finish with meringue close to serving.

Nice lemon meringue pie

PREP TIME 30 MINS **COOK TIME** 7 MINS **FRIDGE TIME** 20 MINS

A citrus and meringue classic with a delicious Arnott's base. Make sure you grate the lemon zest before you squeeze the juice, it's so much easier.

BISCUIT BASE
250g pkt Arnott's Nice biscuits
125g unsalted butter, melted

LEMON CURD
½ cup (75g) cornflour
1 cup (220g) caster sugar
½ cup (125ml) lemon juice
2 tsp finely grated lemon zest
100g unsalted butter, chopped
3 egg yolks

MERINGUE TOPPING
3 egg whites
⅔ cup (150g) caster sugar

1 Grease a 24cm loose-based tart tin.

2 Biscuit Base: Place Nice Biscuits in the bowl of a food processor and pulse until fine crumbs form. Add melted butter and process until just combined. Press mixture firmly into the base and side of tin, smoothing the surface. Cover and refrigerate for 20 minutes or until firm.

3 Lemon Curd: Combine cornflour and sugar in a saucepan, gradually stir in juice and 1¼ cups (310ml) water until smooth. Cook over medium-low heat, stirring for 3–4 minutes until mixture boils and thickens. Reduce heat and simmer, stirring for 1 minute. Remove from heat, stir in lemon zest, butter and egg yolks. Cool for 10 minutes.

4 Preheat oven to 220°C fan-forced. Spread cooled curd over biscuit base.

5 Meringue Topping: In the bowl of an electric mixer, beat egg whites until soft peaks form. Add caster sugar 1 spoonful at a time, beating well between additions. Beat for 10 minutes or until sugar dissolves and meringue is smooth and glossy. Spoon meringue over lemon curd.

6 Bake pie for 2 minutes or until the meringue is browned lightly. Cool.

SERVES 10

ARNOTT
MILK COFFEE

No-Bake Delights

Iced VoVo tart

PREP TIME 30 MINS **COOK TIME** 10 MINS **FRIDGE TIME** 4 HRS+

What's better than an Iced Vovo biscuit? Recreating the unmistakable colours and flavours of the iconic biscuit into one irresistible tart!

150ml thickened cream, whipped
shredded coconut, to decorate

BISCUIT BASE

210g pkt Arnott's Iced VoVo biscuits
100g butter, melted

MARSHMALLOW FILLING

100g pink marshmallows
1 tbsp milk
150ml thickened cream

RASPBERRY JELLY

2 tsp gelatine powder
1½ tbsp boiling water
1 cup (150g) frozen raspberries
1 tbsp caster sugar

1 Biscuit Base: Lightly grease a 10cm x 34cm loose-based tart tin. Place Iced VoVo biscuits in the bowl of a food processor and pulse until fine crumbs form. Add melted butter and pulse until combined. Press crumbs firmly over base and sides of tin. Refrigerate for 20 minutes or until firm.

Scan here for a short how-to video making this recipe.

2 Marshmallow Filling: In a small saucepan, stir marshmallows and milk over low heat for 4–5 minutes until the marshmallows melt and mixture is smooth. Transfer to a bowl. Cool for 10 minutes.

3 In a bowl, whisk cream until firm peaks form then stand at room temperature for 10 minutes (this will prevent the mixture from splitting). Add cream to marshmallow mixture and stir gently to combine. Spoon over biscuit base and smooth the surface. Cover and refrigerate for 2 hours.

4 Raspberry Jelly: Meanwhile, place gelatine and boiling water in a small jug; stir until gelatine dissolves. In a small saucepan, cook raspberries, sugar and ⅓ cup (80ml) water over low heat for 2 minutes or until sugar dissolves. Bring to a simmer, cook for a further 2 minutes or until raspberries have softened. Remove from heat and stir in gelatine mixture. Strain mixture through a sieve into a jug, discard seeds. Cool slightly, cover and refrigerate for 20 minutes or until slightly thickened and the consistency of pouring cream. Carefully pour jelly over filling. Cover and refrigerate for 2 hours until set.

5 Place whipped cream into a piping bag fitted with a 1cm star nozzle. Pipe 2 rows of cream along each long side of the tart. Sprinkle tart with shredded coconut.

SERVES 12

A TIP FROM

Chef Ness

When cutting the slice into pieces, wipe the knife clean between cuts to prevent crumbs sticking to the jelly layer.

Scotch Finger jelly slice

PREP TIME 15 MINS **FRIDGE TIME** 4 HRS+

This nostalgic slice is a great one to get the kids involved in the kitchen. Just make sure they don't eat it all before it sets.

BISCUIT BASE

250g pkt Arnott's Scotch Finger biscuits (or 250g Arnott's Gluten Free Scotch Finger biscuits)

150g butter, melted

LEMON FILLING

395g can sweetened condensed milk

½ cup (125ml) lemon juice

1½ tsp gelatine powder

½ cup (125ml) boiling water

JELLY TOPPING

85g pkt raspberry jelly crystals (ensure gluten free, if required)

1 Grease an 18cm x 28cm slice tin, line base and sides with baking paper, extending paper 5cm above edge of tin.

2 Biscuit Base: Place Scotch Finger biscuits in the bowl of a food processor and pulse until fine crumbs form. Add melted butter and process until just combined. Press mixture firmly into base of tin, smoothing the surface with a spoon or flat-based glass. Cover and refrigerate for 20 minutes or until firm.

3 Lemon Filling: In a medium bowl, combine condensed milk and lemon juice; mix well. Combine gelatine and boiling water in a small jug; stir until gelatine dissolves. Cool slightly. Stir into milk mixture; pour over biscuit base. Cover and refrigerate for 2 hours or until firm.

4 Jelly Topping: Prepare jelly according to packet instructions using 100ml less cold water than directed. Refrigerate jelly for 20 minutes or until slightly thickened and the consistency of pouring cream. Pour over lemon filling. Cover and refrigerate for 2 hours or until set.

5 Cut into pieces before serving.

MAKES 12

Choc Ripple peanut butter cheesecake

PREP TIME 15 MINS **COOK TIME** 2 MINS **FRIDGE TIME** 4 HRS+

If you've been searching for the best chilled cheesecake ever, then look no further! This combination of peanut butter and chocolate is a winner.

BISCUIT BASE

250g pkt Arnott's Choc Ripple biscuits (or 250g Arnott's Gluten Free Scotch Finger biscuits)

100g unsalted butter, melted

CREAM CHEESE FILLING

3 tsp gelatine powder

¼ cup (60ml) boiling water

500g cream cheese, softened

¾ cup (165g) caster sugar

⅓ cup (95g) smooth peanut butter

300ml thickened cream

CHOCOLATE TOPPING

180g dark chocolate, chopped

¼ cup (70g) smooth or crunchy peanut butter

1 Grease and line base of a 22cm (base measure) springform tin with baking paper.

2 Biscuit Base: Place Choc Ripple biscuits in the bowl of a food processor and pulse until fine crumbs form. Add melted butter and pulse until combined. Press mixture firmly into base of tin, smoothing the surface with a spoon or flat-based glass. Cover and refrigerate for 20 minutes or until firm.

3 Cream Cheese Filling: Place gelatine and boiling water in a small jug, stir until gelatine dissolves. In the bowl of an electric mixer, beat cream cheese and sugar for 2–3 minutes until smooth. Add peanut butter and beat to combine. Pour in cream, beat for 1 minute until slightly thickened. Add gelatine mixture and beat on low for 1 minute until mixed through. Pour mixture over biscuit base. Cover and refrigerate for 2 hours or until just set.

4 Chocolate Topping: Place chocolate and peanut butter in a microwave-safe bowl. Microwave for 1–2 minutes on medium power, stirring every 30 seconds until melted and smooth. Pour evenly over cheesecake. Cover and refrigerate for 2 hours or until set.

SERVES 10

Tim Tam fudgy slice

PREP TIME 15 MINS **COOK TIME** 8 MINS **FRIDGE TIME** 4 HRS+

Using just a handful of ingredients, this fudgy chocolate treat is decadent and perfect with a cup of tea or coffee. Just try and stop at one piece.

2 x 200g pkts Arnott's Tim Tam Original biscuits (or 400g Arnott's Gluten Free Tim Tam Original biscuits)
100g butter, chopped
395g can sweetened condensed milk
200g milk chocolate, finely chopped
sea salt flakes, to serve

1 Grease and line an 18cm x 28cm slice tin with baking paper, extending the paper 2cm above the edges.

2 Place 200g (1 pkt) Tim Tam biscuits in the bowl of a food processor and pulse until crumbs form. Transfer to a medium bowl. Roughly chop remaining biscuits.

3 In a small saucepan, stir butter and half the condensed milk over medium heat for 3 minutes or until melted and combined.

4 Pour the butter mixture into bowl of biscuit crumbs, stir well. Add the chopped biscuits and mix well. Spoon mixture into tin, pressing firmly into base and smoothing the surface. Cover and refrigerate for 30 minutes or until firm.

5 In a small saucepan, stir chocolate and remaining condensed milk continuously, over low heat for 5 minutes or until melted and smooth. Pour mixture over biscuit base. Cover and refrigerate for 4 hours or until set.

6 Scatter with salt flakes and cut into fingers before serving.

MAKES 18

A TIP FROM

Chef Ness

Store slice in an airtight container in the fridge for up to 1 week.

Scotch Finger lemon cheesecake slice

PREP TIME 10 MINS **FRIDGE TIME** 4 HRS+

This recipe uses just four ingredients to create a creamy, citrusy family favourite. Make sure to grate the lemon before you squeeze out the juice. Store the slice it in an airtight container in the fridge for up to 3 days.

250g pkt Arnott's Scotch Finger biscuits (or 250g Arnott's Gluten Free Scotch Finger biscuits)
zested lemon rind, to decorate

LEMON FILLING

250g cream cheese, softened
395g can sweetened condensed milk
1 tsp finely grated lemon zest
⅓ cup (80ml) lemon juice

1 Grease and line an 18cm x 28cm slice tin with baking paper, extending the paper 2cm above edge of tin.

2 Arrange 12 Scotch Finger biscuits on base of tin. Finely chop the remaining 2 biscuits and set aside.

3 Lemon Filling: In the bowl of an electric mixer, beat cream cheese, condensed milk, lemon zest and juice for 3 minutes or until well combined and smooth. Spread mixture evenly over the biscuit base. Cover and refrigerate for 4 hours or overnight until firm.

4 Scatter top with the chopped biscuits and zested lemon rind. Cut into pieces before serving.

MAKES 12

A TIP FROM

Chef Ness

Because there is no gelatine in this slice, the texture will be on the slightly (but still delicious) softer side.

A TIP FROM
Chef Ness

Store slice in an airtight container in the fridge for up to 5 days.

Nice lemon slice

PREP TIME 15 MINS **COOK TIME** 8 MINS **FRIDGE TIME** 3 HRS+

You'll be going back for more with this lovely lemon slice. The fudgey buttery base smothered in a zesty icing, is sure to please everyone.

250g pkt Arnott's Nice biscuits
90g butter, chopped
½ cup (120g) sweetened condensed milk
1 tsp finely grated lemon zest
1 tbsp lemon juice

LEMON ICING
1¼ cups (200g) icing sugar
15g butter
1 tbsp lemon juice

1 Grease and line an 18cm x 28cm slice tin with baking paper, extending paper 5cm above edge of tin.

2 Place 200g Nice biscuits in the bowl of a food processor and pulse until fine crumbs form; transfer to a bowl. Chop remaining biscuits coarsely then add to same bowl.

3 In a small saucepan, stir butter, condensed milk, lemon zest and juice over medium-low heat for 4–5 minutes until melted and smooth.

4 Pour butter mixture over biscuit mixture and stir until well combined. Press mixture firmly into base of tin, smoothing the surface with a spoon or flat-based glass. Cover and refrigerate for 1 hour or until just firm.

5 Lemon Icing: Place icing sugar, butter and lemon juice in a heatproof bowl, stir over a saucepan of simmering water for 2–3 minutes until mixture is smooth.

6 Pour icing evenly over slice. Cover and refrigerate for 2 hours or until set.

7 Cut into pieces before serving.

MAKES 20

4 ways Choc Ripple logs

Choc Ripple log

PREP TIME 25 MINS **FRIDGE TIME** 8 HRS+ **SERVES** 8–10

In the bowl of an electric mixer, whisk 600ml thickened cream until firm peaks form. Reserve a third of the cream, refrigerate. Spread a little cream in a line on a serving plate. Using a 250g pkt Choc Ripple biscuits, spread 2 tsp of cream on the flat side of a biscuit and sandwich with another biscuit. Spread another 2 tsp of cream on top of the biscuit sandwich. Place biscuit sandwich on its side over the cream on the plate. Repeat with remaining biscuits and more cream to form a log; spread remaining cream all over the log. Refrigerate for 8 hrs or overnight. To serve, spread reserved cream all over log. Decorate finished log with one of the Toppings opposite.

Toppings

Choc Ripple Tiramisu Before making the log, dissolve 2 tbsp instant coffee and 1 tbsp caster sugar in 2 tbsp boiling water. Brush biscuits with coffee mixture before spreading with cream. Decorate finished log with dark chocolate curls, then dust with cocoa powder.

Scan here for a short how-to video making Choc Ripple Caramel Popcorn log.

Choc Ripple Lolly Decorate finished log with pink and white mini marshmallows, sliced musk sticks and fancy pink sprinkles.

Choc Ripple Caramel Popcorn Decorate finished log with caramel popcorn, then drizzle with caramel sauce.

Choc Ripple Berry Decorate finished log with raspberries and halved strawberries.

Tim Tam mini cheesecakes

PREP TIME 30 MINS **FRIDGE TIME** 4 HRS+

These individual cheesecakes make a decadent single-serve dessert. Make the cheesecakes well ahead of time and keep them in the fridge until you're ready to decorate with cream and extra Tim Tams.

- 200g pkt Arnott's Tim Tam Original biscuits (or 200g Arnott's Gluten Free Tim Tam Original biscuits)
- 80g butter, softened
- 300ml thickened cream
- 250g cream cheese, softened
- ⅓ cup (55g) icing sugar mixture (ensure gluten free, if required), sifted

Scan here for a short how-to video making this recipe.

1 Line a 12-hole (⅓-cup/80ml) muffin tin with paper cases.

2 Place 7 Tim Tam Original biscuits in the bowl of a food processor and pulse until fine crumbs form. Add butter and process until just combined. Spoon mixture evenly into paper cases, pressing firmly into the base. Cover and refrigerate for 20 minutes or until firm.

3 Finely chop 2 biscuits and reserve remaining. In a bowl, whisk half the cream until firm peaks form.

4 In the bowl of an electric mixer, beat cream cheese for 3 minutes or until smooth and light. Add sifted icing sugar mixture and beat until combined. Using a large metal spoon, fold the whipped cream and chopped Tim Tams into cream cheese mixture until combined.

5 Spoon mixture evenly into paper cases onto biscuit bases, smooth the top. Cover and refrigerate for 4 hours or until set.

6 Just before serving, cut reserved biscuits into slices. In a bowl, whisk remaining cream until firm peaks form. Dollop cream onto cheesecakes and decorate with sliced biscuits.

MAKES 12

Hedgehog slice

PREP TIME 15 MINS **COOK TIME** 5 MINS **FRIDGE TIME** 2 HRS+

You will have 6 Milk Coffee biscuits left over from a 250g packet, simply keep these for another use or just to snack on with a good cuppa.

200g Arnott's Milk Coffee biscuits
175g unsalted butter, chopped
80g dark chocolate, chopped
¾ cup (90g) walnuts, finely chopped
1 tbsp cocoa powder, sifted

CHOCOLATE TOPPING
200g dark chocolate, chopped
20g butter

1 Grease and line an 18cm x 28cm slice tin with baking paper, extending the paper 2cm above edge of tin.

2 Place 100g Milk Coffee biscuits in the bowl of a food processor and pulse until fine crumbs form; transfer to a bowl. Finely chop another 100g biscuits then add to same bowl. (You will have 6 biscuits left in the packet, save these for another use.)

3 In a small saucepan, stir butter and chocolate over low heat for 3 minutes or until melted and smooth. Pour butter mixture over biscuit mixture then add the walnuts and cocoa; stir until well combined. Press mixture firmly into tin. Cover and refrigerate for 1 hour or until just firm.

4 Chocolate Topping: Place chocolate and butter in a microwave-safe bowl. Microwave for 1–2 minutes on medium power, stirring every 30 seconds until melted and smooth. Pour topping evenly over slice. Cover and refrigerate for 1 hour or until set.

5 Cut into pieces before serving.

MAKES 18

A TIP FROM Chef Ness

Store slice in an airtight container in the fridge for up to 5 days.

Butternut Snap Easter tartlets

PREP TIME 10 MINS **COOK TIME** 15 MINS

Patty pans have a rounded base and hold 1½ tablespoons. To make the cup shape bases for the tartlets, use a small ladle or whole fresh lime to gently push down on the softened biscuits, moulding them to the rounded holes.

250g pkt Arnott's Butternut Snap Cookie
21 small milk chocolate Easter eggs

CHOCOLATE FILLING

⅓ cup (80ml) thickened cream
200g dark chocolate, chopped
65g unsalted butter, chopped

1 Preheat oven to 180°C fan-forced.

2 Place a Butternut Snap Cookie over each hole of a 12-hole round-based patty pan. Place in oven for 2–3 minutes until softened. Remove from oven then carefully press softened biscuits into holes moulding into a cup shape. Cool in pan. Transfer cooled biscuits to a tray. Repeat with remaining biscuits.

3 Chocolate Filling: In a saucepan, combine cream, chocolate and butter stirring continuously over low heat for 6–8 minutes until melted and smooth. Pour into a heatproof bowl to cool slightly.

4 Spoon chocolate filling into each biscuit cup and top each with an Easter egg pressing gently into the filling. Refrigerate until set.

MAKES 21

A TIP FROM

Chef Ness

Remove ice-cream cake from freezer 5 minutes before serving, this will make it easier to cut into slices.

FF

Mint Slice ice-cream cake

PREP TIME 20 MINS **FREEZE TIME** 12 HRS+

The perfect family summer treat, this ice-cream cake contains only three ingredients (well, four if you count the mint leaves on top!), making it super easy and quick to put together. Keep one in the freezer on standby!

2 x 200g pkts Arnott's Mint Slice biscuits (or 400g Gluten Free Arnott's Mint Slice biscuits)
600ml thickened cream
395g can sweetened condensed milk
fresh mint leaves, to decorate

1 Line the base of a 22cm (base measure) springform tin with baking paper.

2 Using 200g (1 pkt) Mint Slice biscuits, place biscuits around the inside of the tin, with the top-side of each biscuit facing the side of the tin. Chop the remaining biscuits and set aside.

3 In the bowl of an electric mixer, beat cream and condensed milk for 3–4 minutes or until firm peaks form.

4 Add the chopped biscuits to cream mixture, stir well to combine. Pour mixture into tin, smoothing the surface with the back of a spoon. Cover and freeze for 12 hours or overnight.

5 To serve, remove ice-cream cake from tin (see tip); place on a platter and decorate with fresh mint leaves.

SERVES 8–10

Happy
Birthdays

Campfire cake

PREP TIME 30 MINS **COOK TIME** 10 MINS

If you're going for a camping themed party, make sure to add any (or all) of the three s'mores on page 36 to the menu. The kids will love it.

600g store-bought chocolate mud cake
175g pkt Arnott's TeeVee Snacks Malt Sticks
3 Arnott's Tim Tam Original biscuits, cut in half, lengthways
mini marshmallows and cocktail sticks, to decorate

CHOCOLATE BUTTERCREAM

125g butter, softened
1½ cups (240g) icing sugar, sifted
2 tbsp cocoa powder, sifted
1 tbsp milk, approximately

TOFFEE FLAMES

½ cup (110g) caster sugar
orange gel food colouring

1 Chocolate Buttercream: In the bowl of an electric mixer, beat butter until pale. Gradually add sifted icing sugar and cocoa until combined. Beat in enough milk to soften for a spreadable consistency.

2 Toffee Flames: Line a tray with baking paper. Place sugar and ¼ cup (60ml) water in a small saucepan, stir over low heat until sugar dissolves. Bring mixture to the boil; boil uncovered, without stirring, until mixture is light caramel in colour. Remove from heat, working quickly pour 1 tablespoon of mixture onto the lined tray, squeeze a small drop of orange colour into the middle. Using a skewer pull the colour through the toffee to create flames. Repeat with remaining toffee and more colouring. Allow to set then place in an airtight container until needed.

3 When ready to serve, place cake on a serving board. Spread buttercream over top and side of cake. Place TeeVee Snacks Malt Sticks around side of cake. Tie 3 Malt Sticks with string for a bundle of logs. Press toffee flames into cake for the fire. Place halved Tim Tams around flames for logs. Place a marshmallow on the end of each cocktail stick and position on and around the cake.

SERVES 8

A TIP FROM

Chef Ness

A white chocolate mud cake or caramel mud cake could easily be used instead of the chocolate mud cake.

A TIP FROM

Chef Ness

Pour jelly over the back of a spoon when pouring it over the lemon filling to ensure a smooth base.

Tiny Teddy beach cake

PREP TIME 30 MINS **FRIDGE TIME** 5 HRS+

Make a splash and take your birthday party to the beach with this fun sea-side cake, complete with biscuit crumb sand and blue jelly water.

BISCUIT BASE
250g pkt Arnott's Milk Arrowroot biscuits
150g butter, melted

LEMON FILLING
395g can sweetened condensed milk
½ cup (125ml) lemon juice
1½ tsp gelatine powder
½ cup (125ml) boiling water

JELLY LAYER
2 x 85g pkt Berry Blue jelly

TO DECORATE
Arnott's Tiny Teddy Honey biscuits
Arnott's Tiny Teddy Chocolate biscuits
jelly rings, sour straps and cocktail umbrellas

1 Grease and line a 20cm (base measure) springform tin with baking paper.

2 Biscuit base: Place Milk Arrowroot biscuits in the bowl of food processor and pulse until fine crumbs form. Add melted butter and pulse until combined. Reserve ⅓ cup crumb mixture. Press remaining mixture firmly into base of tin. Cover and refrigerate for 20 minutes or until firm.

3 Lemon Filling: In a bowl, combine condensed milk and lemon juice, stir well. Combine gelatine and boiling water in a small jug; stir until gelatine dissolves. Cool slightly. Pour gelatine mixture into condensed milk mixture and stir well. Pour filling over biscuit base. Cover and refrigerate for 3 hours or until set.

4 Jelly Layer: Meanwhile, prepare jelly according to packet instructions, using 200ml less cold water than directed. Stand 30 minutes at room temperature to cool. When slightly thickened, pour mixture over set filling (see tip).

5 Cover and refrigerate for a further 2 hours or until jelly is set. When ready to decorate, remove cake from tin and transfer to a serving board. Scatter reserved crumbs on one side of jelly and on board for sand. Arrange Tiny Teddy biscuits, jelly rings, sour straps and umbrellas as shown.

SERVES 12

Milk Coffee chocolate layer cake

PREP TIME 10 MINS **COOK TIME** 8 MINS **FRIDGE TIME** 8 HRS+

With just four ingredients, this simple but elegant layer cake can be enjoyed at any occasion.

395g can sweetened condensed milk
100g unsalted butter, chopped
225g dark chocolate Melts
250g pkt Arnott's Milk Coffee biscuits

1 Grease and line a 7cm x 9cm x 18cm (base measure) loaf tin with baking paper, extending the paper 5cm above edges.

2 In a medium saucepan, stir condensed milk, butter and chocolate over low heat for 3 minutes or until melted. Simmer gently, constantly stirring, for 5–6 minutes until mixture thickens slightly. Watch closely to avoid mixture catching on the pan. Stand for 5 minutes to cool slightly.

3 Pour ⅓ cup chocolate mixture into the base of tin. Top with 4 Milk Coffee biscuits. Repeat with remaining chocolate mixture and biscuits until you have 6 layers of biscuits. Top with remaining chocolate mixture. Cover and refrigerate for 8 hours or overnight.

4 To serve, turn cake out onto a serving platter and cut into slices.

SERVES 12

A TIP FROM

Chef Ness

Refrigerating the tiramisu for 8 hours or overnight allows the biscuits to soften and soak in the coffee flavour.

Scotch Finger tiramisu

PREP TIME 20 MINS **FRIDGE TIME** 8 HRS+

Scotch Finger biscuits are meant to be dunked, so here's one for the coffee lovers! Soak these iconic biscuits in coffee to soften, then layer them with lashings of creamy mascarpone mixture. It's the perfect pick me up.

250g pkt Arnott's Scotch Finger biscuits (or 250g Arnott's Gluten Free Scotch Finger biscuits)
2 tbsp instant coffee
2 tbsp caster sugar
200ml boiling water
300ml thickened cream
250g mascarpone
1 tbsp cocoa powder
fresh raspberries, to decorate

1 Line base and sides of a 7cm x 9cm x 18cm (base measure) loaf tin with baking paper, extending paper 2cm above edges.

2 Reserve 2 Scotch Finger biscuits. Combine coffee and sugar with boiling water, stir until sugar dissolves. Set aside to cool slightly.

3 In the bowl of an electric mixer, beat cream until soft peaks form. Using a large whisk, gently fold the mascarpone into the cream until combined and smooth (overwhisking will cause it to split).

4 Spread ½ cup (125ml) cream mixture on base of lined tin. Take 4 Scotch Finger biscuits and soak each biscuit in the coffee mixture until they start to soften. Place biscuits in one layer on cream base in tin, sift over 1 teaspoon of the cocoa. Repeat layering two more times with ½ cup cream mixture, soaked biscuits and cocoa, finishing with a layer of the remaining cream mixture and cocoa. Cover and refrigerate for 8 hours or overnight.

5 Coarsely chop reserved biscuits. When ready to serve, lift tiramisu out of the tin and transfer to a serving platter. Decorate with chopped biscuits and raspberries. Cut into slices with a sharp knife.

SERVES 10

Scotch Finger lemon tart

PREP TIME 25 MINS **COOK TIME** 45 MINS **FRIDGE TIME** 30 MINS+

Full of zesty freshness, this luscious tart benefits from being made a day ahead. It will develop a more intense flavour if left overnight in the fridge.

blueberries and sifted icing sugar (gluten free, as required), to serve

BISCUIT BASE

250g pkt Arnott's Scotch Finger biscuits (or 250g Arnott's Gluten Free Scotch Finger biscuits)

100g unsalted butter, melted

LEMON FILLING

6 eggs

¾ cup (165g) caster sugar

300ml thickened cream

1 tbsp finely grated lemon zest

¾ cup (125ml) lemon juice

1 Preheat oven to 160°C fan-forced.

2 Biscuit Base: Place biscuits in the bowl of a food processor and process until fine crumbs form. Add melted butter and process until combined. Press mixture firmly into the base and side of a 4cm deep, 24cm (base measure) round loose-based tart tin. Place on an oven tray and bake for 15 minutes.

3 Lemon Filling: In a large bowl, gently whisk eggs, sugar, cream, lemon zest and juice until combined and sugar dissolves. Stand for 5 minutes for bubbles to settle. Pour filling over biscuit base.

4 Bake tart for 30 minutes or until filling is just set. Transfer to a wire rack to cool. Cover and refrigerate until ready to serve.

5 Serve tart topped with blueberries and dusted with icing sugar.

SERVES 8–10

ARNOTT
SCOTCH

Tina Wafer ice-cream sundae

PREP TIME 5 MINUTES

An ice-cream sundae is fun for the whole family. For more adult flavours, you can use scoops of coffee, salted caramel and vanilla bean ice-creams, before topping with chocolate sauce and Arnott's Tina Wafer biscuits.

6 scoops Neapolitan ice-cream
⅓ cup (80ml) bottled strawberry sauce
6 Arnott's Tina Wafer biscuits

1 Place a scoop each of strawberry, chocolate and vanilla ice-cream into each of 2 sundae glasses or bowls.

2 Drizzle with strawberry sauce and top with Tina Wafer biscuits.

SERVES 2

Arnott's semi-trailer truck cake

PREP TIME 1 HR

4 x 450g Madeira cakes
2 bamboo skewers
20cm x 60cm cake board

BUTTERCREAM

250g butter, softened
3 cups (480g) icing sugar, sifted
1-2 tbsp milk, approximately
red gel food colouring

DECORATIONS

Arnottt's TeeVee Snacks Malt Sticks
Arnott's Mint Slice biscuits
Arnott's Tina Wafer biscuits
Arnott's Gaiety biscuits
2 Arnott's Tiny Teddy biscuits
licorice straps
yellow chocolate buttons
2 long red birthday candles

1 Buttercream: In the bowl of an electric mixer, beat butter until white as possible. Gradually add half the icing sugar, beating continually. Gradually add half the milk and remaining icing sugar. Add enough remaining milk to achieve a smooth consistency. Add enough red food colouring for a deep Arnott's Red colour. Place ½ cup buttercream in a small piping bag.

2 Trim sides and top of madeira cakes so they are level. Spread tops of 2 cakes with buttercream. Cut 1 remaining cake in half horizontally, place each half on top of buttercream to make 2 sandwiched cakes. For the cab, cut a 5cm thick slice from remaining madeira cake. Spread buttercream on base of cake slice and place onto top end of cut cake, as shown; secure with 2 skewers.

3 Place sandwiched cakes on the board. Spread buttercream all over the trailer. Position cab cakes in front of trailer on board and spread buttercream all over. Place candles at the back of the cab for exhaust pipes.

4 Pipe a little buttercream on chocolate buttons and stick one in the middle of each Mint Slice biscuit; place biscuits along base of cake as shown for wheels. Stick 2 chocolate buttons on the front of engine for headlights. Decorate with licorice strap for the wheel hubs, bumper, grill and trim on truck as shown. Place 2 Tina Wafers on the front of the cab and 2 Tina Wafer halves on the side of cab for windows. Pipe a little buttercream onto smooth side of Tiny Teddy biscuits and stick to the front windows, pipe icing on the teddys for a seat belt.

5 Fill the trailer with Malt Sticks, Tina Wafer biscuits and Gaiety biscuits.

SERVES 30

A TIP FROM

Chef Ness

Add another trailer to the truck to make a B-double if you are feeding a lot of kids. Cake can be decorated several hours ahead, arrange biscuits close to serving to prevent the biscuits from going soft.

A TIP FROM
Chef Ness
The cake can be made 1 day ahead. Decorate cake on day of celebration.

Hundreds & Thousands princess birthday cake

PREP TIME 10 MINS **COOK TIME** 1 HR 15 MINS

A pretty pink princess is the childhood dream birthday cakes are made for! And no matter our age, there's a touch of royalty in all of us.

1 doll
2 x 200g pkt Arnott's Hundreds & Thousands biscuits
long silver candles, to decorate

CAKE
2 x 440g Butter cake mix
4 eggs
120g butter, softened
300ml milk

BUTTERCREAM
250g salted butter, softened
3 cups (480g) icing sugar mixture
pink food colouring
1 tbsp milk, approximately

1 Cake: Preheat oven to 150°C fan-forced. Grease and line base of a Dolly Varden cake tin.

2 Make cakes in one batch following the packet directions. Pour into tin and bake for 1¼ hours or until a skewer inserted in the centre comes out clean. Stand in tin for 10 minutes before turning out onto a wire rack to cool.

3 Buttercream: In the bowl of an electric mixer, beat butter for 5 minutes or until pale in colour. Gradually add sifted icing sugar, beating constantly between additions, until light and fluffy. Spoon ½ cup buttercream into a piping bag fitted with a fluted piping tip.

4 Add food colour a little at a time to remaining buttercream until pale pink. Add milk gradually to soften buttercream as needed. Spoon one-third of the pink buttercream into another piping bag fitted with a fluted piping tip.

5 When cake is cool, gently push doll down into the centre through the top of cake. Spread pink buttercream evenly over cake. Arrange Hundreds & Thousands biscuits, slightly overlapping over cake.

6 Pipe pink buttercream around top of biscuit skirt and plain buttercream around base of biscuit skirt. Position candles.

SERVES 16

4 ways Tiny Teddy adventures

Tiny Teddy Goes Skiing

Place 24 TeeVee Snacks Malt Sticks biscuits side-by-side in twos on a baking-paper-lined tray. Tint 60g melted white chocolate Melts with red gel food colouring and tint another 60g melted white chocolate Melts with orange gel food colouring. Dip the bottom half of a Tiny Teddy into one of the chocolates, place upright on Malt Sticks, hold for a few seconds to set. Repeat with 11 more Tiny Teddys, dipping half into each colour. Serve skiing teddy on scoops of vanilla ice-cream. MAKES 12

Tiny Teddy Goes To Bed

Melt 100g white chocolate Melts. Paint a little chocolate onto the back of 1 or 2 Tiny Teddy biscuits and stick them on top of a Hundreds & Thousands biscuit. Stand for 5 minutes to set. Dip bottom half of biscuits into melted chocolate to represent a blanket. Place on baking-paper-lined tray to set. Repeat to make 24 in total. Refrigerate until set. MAKES 24

Tiny Teddy Goes Driving

Using a small sharp knife, cut a small indent into 12 Gaiety biscuits for teddy's feet. Dip a Tiny Teddy biscuit halfway into 100g melted milk chocolate Melts. Place in indent, hold for a few seconds to set. Dip 1 side of 4 fruit tingles (same colour) into chocolate and secure to Gaiety biscuit for wheels. Dip cut side of a halved fruit tingle into chocolate, place in front of teddy for steering wheel, hold briefly to set. Repeat with remaining biscuits, chocolate and 54 fruit tingles. Refrigerate until set. MAKES 12

Tiny Teddy Goes Rafting

Place 36 TeeVee Snacks Malt Sticks biscuits side-by-side in threes on a baking-paper-lined tray. Working one at a time, dip the side of 2 Malt Sticks in 100g melted milk chocolate Melts, stick together with a third Malt Stick to form a raft. Dip the bottom half of a Tiny Teddy biscuit in 60g melted white chocolate Melts, place upright on raft, hold for a few seconds to set. Refrigerate until set. MAKES 12

Scotch Finger macaroon cake

PREP TIME 20 MINS **COOK TIME** 25 MINS

When a birthday celebration calls for something elegant, this macaroon cake is at the top of the list. Topped with fresh fruit, it will surely delight.

- 250g pkt Arnott's Scotch Finger biscuits (or 250g Arnott's Gluten Free Scotch Finger biscuits)
- 3 egg whites
- ⅔ cup (150g) caster sugar
- 1 cup (80g) desiccated coconut
- 600ml thickened cream
- 1 tbsp icing sugar (ensure gluten free, if required)
- ¼ cup (60ml) passionfruit pulp
- fresh raspberries and mint leaves, to decorate

1 Preheat oven to 150°C fan-forced. Lightly grease two oven trays. Mark an 18cm circle on two sheets of baking paper; place papers marked-side down on trays.

2 Place Scotch Finger biscuits in the bowl of a food processor and process until fine crumbs form. Set aside.

3 In the bowl of an electric mixer, beat egg whites and sugar for 8–10 minutes until meringue is thick and glossy. Using a large metal spoon, fold in biscuit crumbs and coconut. Spread mixture inside the two marked circles.

4 Bake for 25 minutes until just golden and firm. Cool on trays.

5 Meanwhile, in the bowl of an electric mixer, whisk cream and icing sugar until firm peaks form.

6 Place one macaroon circle on a serving plate. Spread with half the cream mixture. Drizzle with half the passionfruit. Top with remaining macaroon circle, cream mixture and passionfruit. Decorate with raspberries and mint leaves.

SERVES 10

A TIP FROM

Chef Ness

Cake can be made to the end of step 4 up to 2 days ahead. Store in an airtight container in a cool dry place. Assemble close to serving.

Tim Tam ganache tart

PREP TIME 30 MINS **COOK TIME** 4 MINS **FRIDGE TIME** 2 HRS+

Calling all chocolate lovers! This sophisticated tart contains three layers of chocolatey deliciousness, making it a truly decadent dessert.

cocoa powder, to serve

BISCUIT BASE

2 x 200g pkts Arnott's Tim Tam Original biscuits (or 400g Arnott's Gluten Free Tim Tam Original biscuits)

40g butter, softened

MILK CHOCOLATE GANACHE

350g milk chocolate, chopped

200ml thickened cream

30g butter

½ tsp sea salt flakes

DARK CHOCOLATE GANACHE

100g dark chocolate, chopped

30g butter

1 Grease a 2.5cm x 11cm x 35cm loose-based tart tin.

2 Biscuit Base: Reserve 5 Tim Tam biscuits. Add remaining biscuits to the bowl of a food processor and pulse until fine crumbs form. Add butter and process until just combined. Press mixture firmly over the base and sides of tin. Cover and refrigerate for 20 minutes or until firm.

3 Milk Chocolate Ganache: Place the milk chocolate, cream, butter and sea salt in a microwave-safe bowl. Microwave for 2–3 minutes on medium power, stirring every 30 seconds until melted and smooth. Set aside for 5 minutes to cool slightly. Pour over the biscuit base. Cover and refrigerate for 2 hours or until just set.

4 Dark Chocolate Ganache: Place the dark chocolate and butter in a microwave-safe bowl. Microwave for 1–2 minutes on medium power, stirring every 30 seconds until melted and smooth. Set aside for 5 minutes to cool slightly. Pour over the milk chocolate ganache, spreading it out to the edges. Cover and refrigerate for 30 minutes or until set.

5 Cut the reserved biscuits crosswise into pieces. Transfer tart to a serving plate, decorate with biscuit pieces and dust with sifted cocoa.

SERVES 10

CONVERSION CHART

MEASURES

One Australian metric measuring cup holds approximately 250ml; one Australian metric tablespoon holds 20ml; one Australian metric teaspoon holds 5ml. The difference between one country's measuring cups and another's is within a two- or three-teaspoon variance and will not affect your cooking results. North America, New Zealand and the United Kingdom use a 15ml tablespoon. All cup and spoon measurements are level.

The most accurate way of measuring dry ingredients is to weigh them. When measuring liquids, use a clear glass or plastic jug with metric markings.

We use extra-large eggs with an average weight of 60g.

DRY MEASURES

metric	imperial
15g	½oz
30g	1oz
60g	2oz
90g	3oz
125g	4oz (¼lb)
155g	5oz
185g	6oz
220g	7oz
250g	8oz (½lb)
280g	9oz
315g	10oz
345g	11oz
375g	12oz (¾lb)
410g	13oz
440g	14oz
470g	15oz
500g	16oz (1lb)
750g	24oz (1½lb)
1kg	32oz (2lb)

OVEN TEMPERATURES

The temperatures in this book are for fan-forced ovens; for conventional ovens, you will need to increase the temperature by 10-20 degrees.

	°C (Celsius)	°F (Fahrenheit)
Very slow	100	200
Slow	130	260
Moderately slow	150	300
Moderate	160	325
Moderately hot	180	350
Hot	200	400
Very hot	220	425

LIQUID MEASURES

metric	imperial
30ml	1 fluid oz
60ml	2 fluid oz
100ml	3 fluid oz
125ml	4 fluid oz
150ml	5 fluid oz
190ml	6 fluid oz
250ml	8 fluid oz
300ml	10 fluid oz
500ml	16 fluid oz
600ml	20 fluid oz
1000ml (1 litre)	1¾ pints

LENGTH MEASURES

metric	imperial
3mm	⅛in
6mm	¼in
1cm	½in
2cm	¾in
2.5cm	1in
5cm	2in
6cm	2½in
8cm	3in
10cm	4in
13cm	5in
15cm	6in
18cm	7in
20cm	8in
22cm	9in
25cm	10in
28cm	11in
30cm	12in (1ft)

INDEX

First Published in 2025 by Are Media Books, Australia. Reprinted 2026

Chief Executive Officer Jane Huxley
Books Director David Scotto
Creative Director Hannah Blackmore
Managing Editor Stephanie Kistner
Food Editor Bronwen Clark

Photographers Alana Landsberry
Ben Cole, Pablo Martin
Stylists Olivia Blackmore, Sharon Kennedy
Photochefs Rebecca Lyall,
Kathy Knudsen
Hair & Make-up Deborah Munday

Chief Marketing Officer Jenni Dill
Treating Business Director Ranita Cowled
Marketing Director Digital, Media & CX Transformation Caroline Bonpain
Head of Social & PR Francesca Reid
Senior Public Relations Manager
Tessa Conboy
Social & Content Executive
Claire Lendvai
Executive Chef Vanessa Horton

Thank you
Special mention to Sharon Kennedy. Shaz has been an invaluable freelancer at Arnott's for over a decade. Her support has been a tremendous asset to me throughout this time. Thank you, Shaz!

Printed in China by C&C Offset Printing Co. Ltd, China.
A catalogue record for this book is available from the National Library of Australia. ISBN 978-1-76122-200-9

Published by Are Media Books, a division of Are Media Pty Limited,
54 Park St, Sydney; GPO Box 4088, Sydney, NSW 2001, Australia
Ph +61 2 9282 8000 www.aremediabooks.com.au